FRACTIONS WORKBOOK

Grade 4 Math Essentials
Children's Fraction Books

Be encouraged to practice and learn dividing numbers with this Workbook.

Have Fun Learning!

Comparing Fractions

Directions:
Compare the fractions and write >, < or = in the box.

1 $\dfrac{5}{10}$ $\square$ $\dfrac{2}{3}$ **2** $\dfrac{2}{3}$ $\square$ $\dfrac{1}{3}$

3 $\dfrac{3}{4}$ $\square$ $\dfrac{5}{10}$ **4** $\dfrac{1}{2}$ $\square$ $\dfrac{4}{6}$

5 $\dfrac{11}{12}$ $\square$ $\dfrac{9}{12}$ **6** $\dfrac{8}{9}$ $\square$ $\dfrac{5}{11}$

7 $\dfrac{11}{12}$ ☐ $\dfrac{9}{12}$ **8** $\dfrac{8}{9}$ ☐ $\dfrac{5}{11}$

9 $\dfrac{8}{9}$ ☐ $\dfrac{6}{10}$ **10** $\dfrac{3}{4}$ ☐ $\dfrac{4}{5}$

11 $\dfrac{3}{5}$ ☐ $\dfrac{2}{4}$ **12** $\dfrac{5}{8}$ ☐ $\dfrac{5}{9}$

13 $\dfrac{2}{6}$ $\square$ $\dfrac{2}{5}$ **14** $\dfrac{3}{6}$ $\square$ $\dfrac{1}{2}$

15 $\dfrac{1}{7}$ $\square$ $\dfrac{5}{7}$ **16** $\dfrac{2}{5}$ $\square$ $\dfrac{3}{6}$

17 $\dfrac{1}{11}$ $\square$ $\dfrac{5}{12}$ **18** $\dfrac{1}{2}$ $\square$ $\dfrac{4}{7}$

19	$\frac{1}{2}$	☐	$\frac{4}{6}$	**20**	$\frac{4}{5}$	☐	$\frac{7}{12}$
21	$\frac{3}{11}$	☐	$\frac{2}{3}$	**22**	$\frac{10}{11}$	☐	$\frac{9}{10}$
23	$\frac{3}{12}$	☐	$\frac{3}{6}$	**24**	$\frac{2}{10}$	☐	$\frac{4}{8}$

25 $\dfrac{2}{4}$ $\square$ $\dfrac{3}{5}$	**26** $\dfrac{6}{7}$ $\square$ $\dfrac{1}{2}$
27 $\dfrac{1}{7}$ $\square$ $\dfrac{5}{7}$	**28** $\dfrac{6}{9}$ $\square$ $\dfrac{1}{8}$
29 $\dfrac{4}{9}$ $\square$ $\dfrac{3}{9}$	**30** $\dfrac{2}{3}$ $\square$ $\dfrac{1}{4}$

Adding Fractions

Directions:

Add the following fractions and mixed numbers.

1. $\dfrac{2}{3} + \dfrac{4}{5} =$

2. $\dfrac{1}{5} + \dfrac{4}{10} =$

3. $\dfrac{2}{4} + \dfrac{2}{3} =$

4. $\dfrac{1}{2} + \dfrac{1}{4} =$

5. $\dfrac{2}{4} + \dfrac{2}{5} =$

6 $\dfrac{2}{4} + \dfrac{2}{5} =$

7 $\dfrac{8}{10} + \dfrac{2}{4} =$

8 $\dfrac{1}{4} + \dfrac{9}{10} =$

9 $\dfrac{1}{3} + \dfrac{1}{2} =$

10 $\dfrac{2}{3} + \dfrac{8}{10} =$

11. $\dfrac{1}{3} + \dfrac{7}{10} =$

12. $\dfrac{1}{2} + \dfrac{1}{3} =$

13. $\dfrac{3}{5} + \dfrac{1}{3} =$

14. $\dfrac{1}{4} + \dfrac{2}{3} =$

15. $\dfrac{2}{4} + \dfrac{2}{3} =$

16 $\dfrac{4}{10} + \dfrac{1}{2} + \dfrac{2}{3} =$

17 $\dfrac{2}{4} + \dfrac{1}{3} + \dfrac{4}{5} =$

18 $\dfrac{2}{5} + \dfrac{2}{4} + \dfrac{1}{3} =$

19 $\dfrac{3}{10} + \dfrac{1}{2} + \dfrac{3}{4} =$

20 $\dfrac{3}{4} + \dfrac{1}{2} + \dfrac{1}{3} =$

21 $\dfrac{9}{10} + \dfrac{2}{3} + \dfrac{1}{2} =$

22 $\dfrac{1}{3} + \dfrac{7}{10} + \dfrac{1}{5} =$

23 $\dfrac{3}{4} + \dfrac{1}{2} + \dfrac{1}{3} =$

24 $\dfrac{1}{4} + \dfrac{5}{10} + \dfrac{3}{5} =$

25 $\dfrac{6}{10} + \dfrac{1}{2} + \dfrac{2}{3} =$

Subtracting Fractions

Directions:

Find the difference between the fractions.
Reduce all answers to lowest term.

1 $\dfrac{4}{5} - \dfrac{2}{4} =$

2 $\dfrac{4}{5} - \dfrac{1}{3} =$

3 $\dfrac{9}{10} - \dfrac{2}{3} =$

4 $\dfrac{3}{4} - \dfrac{1}{2} =$

5 $\dfrac{1}{2} - \dfrac{2}{5} =$

6 $\dfrac{1}{2} - \dfrac{2}{5} =$

7 $\dfrac{1}{2} - \dfrac{1}{5} =$

8 $\dfrac{2}{4} - \dfrac{1}{2} =$

9 $\dfrac{3}{4} - \dfrac{1}{3} =$

10 $\dfrac{3}{4} - \dfrac{3}{10} =$

11. $\dfrac{5}{10} - \dfrac{1}{4} =$

12. $\dfrac{2}{3} - \dfrac{1}{2} =$

13. $\dfrac{1}{3} - \dfrac{3}{10} =$

14. $\dfrac{2}{3} - \dfrac{1}{2} =$

15. $\dfrac{5}{10} - \dfrac{1}{2} =$

16 $\dfrac{9}{10} - \dfrac{1}{2} - \dfrac{3}{10} =$

17 $\dfrac{4}{5} - \dfrac{1}{5} - \dfrac{1}{5} =$

18 $\dfrac{4}{5} - \dfrac{1}{4} - \dfrac{1}{5} =$

19 $\dfrac{4}{5} - \dfrac{2}{5} - \dfrac{1}{5} =$

20 $\dfrac{8}{10} - \dfrac{2}{5} - \dfrac{1}{5} =$

21 $\dfrac{8}{10} - \dfrac{1}{3} - \dfrac{3}{10} =$

22 $\dfrac{4}{5} - \dfrac{1}{2} - \dfrac{1}{5} =$

23 $\dfrac{4}{5} - \dfrac{1}{3} - \dfrac{1}{5} =$

24 $\dfrac{8}{10} - \dfrac{2}{5} - \dfrac{2}{10} =$

25 $\dfrac{4}{5} - \dfrac{1}{2} - \dfrac{1}{10} =$

Multipying Fractions

Directions:

Find the difference between the fractions.
Reduce all answers to lowest term.

1 $\dfrac{1}{3} \times \dfrac{1}{2} =$

2 $\dfrac{1}{3} \times \dfrac{2}{4} =$

3 $\dfrac{1}{2} \times \dfrac{9}{10} =$

4 $\dfrac{1}{4} \times \dfrac{9}{10} =$

5 $\dfrac{1}{2} \times \dfrac{3}{5} =$

6 $\dfrac{3}{4} \times \dfrac{3}{5} =$

7 $\dfrac{3}{10} \times \dfrac{2}{5} =$

8 $\dfrac{2}{4} \times \dfrac{2}{5} =$

9 $\dfrac{2}{4} \times \dfrac{2}{5} =$

10 $\dfrac{9}{10} \times \dfrac{1}{3} =$

11) $\dfrac{2}{5} \times \dfrac{2}{10} =$

12) $\dfrac{3}{4} \times \dfrac{2}{3} =$

13) $\dfrac{1}{4} \times \dfrac{1}{2} =$

14) $\dfrac{1}{2} \times \dfrac{6}{10} =$

15) $\dfrac{2}{5} \times \dfrac{3}{4} =$

16 $\dfrac{8}{10} \times 8 =$

17 $\dfrac{1}{10} \times 3 =$

18 $\dfrac{2}{10} \times 8 =$

19 $\dfrac{2}{5} \times 2 =$

20 $\dfrac{2}{4} \times 6 =$

21 $\dfrac{2}{4} \times 6 =$

22 $\dfrac{3}{5} \times 8 =$

23 $\dfrac{3}{4} \times 7 =$

24 $\dfrac{2}{3} \times 9 =$

25 $\dfrac{1}{2} \times 8 =$

Dividing Fractions

Directions:

Divide the following fractions.

1 $2\dfrac{1}{10} \div 2\dfrac{3}{5} =$

2 $4\dfrac{3}{4} \div 2\dfrac{1}{5} =$

3 $3\dfrac{3}{4} \div 3\dfrac{1}{5} =$

4 $3\dfrac{2}{3} \div 3\dfrac{1}{2} =$

5 $2\dfrac{3}{5} \div 4\dfrac{1}{2} =$

6 $4\dfrac{1}{2} \div 4\dfrac{2}{5} =$

7 $2\dfrac{1}{2} \div 3\dfrac{1}{3} =$

8 $4\dfrac{1}{2} \div 4\dfrac{2}{3} =$

9 $4\dfrac{1}{2} \div 4\dfrac{2}{3} =$

10 $2\dfrac{1}{2} \div 2\dfrac{1}{2} =$

11. $3\dfrac{1}{2} \div 4\dfrac{1}{3} =$

12. $2\dfrac{3}{4} \div 2\dfrac{4}{5} =$

13. $4\dfrac{1}{2} \div 3\dfrac{1}{3} =$

14. $3\dfrac{1}{2} \div 2\dfrac{2}{5} =$

15. $2\dfrac{1}{2} \div 3\dfrac{3}{5} =$

16. $6 \div \dfrac{4}{5} =$

17. $\dfrac{1}{2} \div 3 =$

18. $8 \div \dfrac{1}{2} =$

19. $6 \div \dfrac{1}{10} =$

20. $7 \div \dfrac{3}{4} =$

21 $\dfrac{3}{10} \div 6 =$

22 $7 \div \dfrac{2}{4} =$

23 $\dfrac{2}{4} \div 9 =$

24 $\dfrac{1}{3} \div 2 =$

25 $\dfrac{1}{5} \div 4 =$

Answers

Comparing Fractions

1. $\frac{5}{10}$ $<$ $\frac{2}{3}$ 2. $\frac{2}{3}$ $>$ $\frac{1}{3}$ 7. $\frac{11}{12}$ $>$ $\frac{9}{12}$ 8. $\frac{8}{9}$ $>$ $\frac{5}{11}$

3. $\frac{3}{4}$ $>$ $\frac{5}{10}$ 4. $\frac{1}{2}$ $<$ $\frac{4}{6}$ 9. $\frac{8}{9}$ $>$ $\frac{6}{10}$ 10. $\frac{3}{4}$ $<$ $\frac{4}{5}$

5. $\frac{11}{12}$ $>$ $\frac{9}{12}$ 6. $\frac{8}{9}$ $>$ $\frac{5}{11}$ 11. $\frac{3}{5}$ $>$ $\frac{2}{4}$ 12. $\frac{5}{8}$ $>$ $\frac{5}{9}$

13. $\frac{2}{6}$ $<$ $\frac{2}{5}$ 14. $\frac{3}{6}$ $=$ $\frac{1}{2}$ 19. $\frac{1}{2}$ $<$ $\frac{4}{6}$ 20. $\frac{4}{5}$ $>$ $\frac{7}{12}$

15. $\frac{1}{7}$ $<$ $\frac{5}{7}$ 16. $\frac{2}{5}$ $<$ $\frac{3}{6}$ 21. $\frac{3}{11}$ $<$ $\frac{2}{3}$ 22. $\frac{10}{11}$ $>$ $\frac{9}{10}$

17. $\frac{1}{11}$ $<$ $\frac{5}{12}$ 18. $\frac{1}{2}$ $<$ $\frac{4}{7}$ 23. $\frac{3}{12}$ $<$ $\frac{3}{6}$ 24. $\frac{2}{10}$ $<$ $\frac{4}{8}$

25. $\frac{2}{4}$ $<$ $\frac{3}{5}$ 26. $\frac{6}{7}$ $>$ $\frac{1}{2}$

27. $\frac{1}{7}$ $<$ $\frac{5}{7}$ 28. $\frac{6}{9}$ $>$ $\frac{1}{8}$

29. $\frac{4}{9}$ $>$ $\frac{3}{9}$ 30. $\frac{2}{3}$ $>$ $\frac{1}{4}$

Adding Fractions

1 $\dfrac{22}{15} =$ $1\dfrac{7}{15}$

2 $\dfrac{6}{10} =$ $\dfrac{3}{5}$

3 $\dfrac{14}{12} =$ $\dfrac{7}{6} =$ $1\dfrac{1}{6}$

4 $\dfrac{3}{4}$

5 $\dfrac{18}{20} =$ $\dfrac{9}{10}$

6 $\dfrac{18}{20} =$ $\dfrac{9}{10}$

7 $\dfrac{26}{20} =$ $\dfrac{13}{10} =$ $1\dfrac{3}{10}$

8 $\dfrac{23}{20} =$ $1\dfrac{3}{20}$

9 $\dfrac{5}{6}$

10 $\dfrac{44}{30} =$ $\dfrac{22}{15} =$ $1\dfrac{7}{15}$

11 $\dfrac{31}{30} =$ $1\dfrac{1}{30}$

12 $\dfrac{5}{6}$

13 $\dfrac{14}{15}$

14 $\dfrac{11}{12}$

15 $\dfrac{14}{12} =$ $\dfrac{7}{6} =$ $1\dfrac{1}{6}$

16 $\dfrac{12}{30} + \dfrac{15}{30} + \dfrac{20}{30} =$ $\dfrac{47}{30} =$ $1\dfrac{17}{30}$

17 $\dfrac{30}{60} + \dfrac{20}{60} + \dfrac{48}{60} =$ $\dfrac{98}{60} =$ $\dfrac{49}{30} =$ $1\dfrac{19}{30}$

18 $\dfrac{24}{60} + \dfrac{30}{60} + \dfrac{20}{60} =$ $\dfrac{74}{60} =$ $\dfrac{37}{30} =$ $1\dfrac{7}{30}$

19 $\dfrac{6}{20} + \dfrac{10}{20} + \dfrac{15}{20} =$ $\dfrac{31}{20} =$ $1\dfrac{11}{20}$

20 $\dfrac{9}{12} + \dfrac{6}{12} + \dfrac{4}{12} =$ $\dfrac{19}{12} =$ $1\dfrac{7}{12}$

21 $\dfrac{62}{30} =$ $\dfrac{31}{15} =$ $2\dfrac{1}{15}$

22 $\dfrac{37}{30} =$ $1\dfrac{7}{30}$

23 $\dfrac{19}{12} =$ $1\dfrac{7}{12}$

24 $\dfrac{27}{20} =$ $1\dfrac{7}{20}$

25 $\dfrac{53}{30} =$ $1\dfrac{23}{30}$

Subtracting Fractions

(1) $\dfrac{16}{20} - \dfrac{10}{20} = \dfrac{6}{20} = \dfrac{3}{10}$

(2) $\dfrac{12}{15} - \dfrac{5}{15} = \dfrac{7}{15}$

(3) $\dfrac{27}{30} - \dfrac{20}{30} = \dfrac{7}{30}$

(4) $\dfrac{3}{4} - \dfrac{2}{4} = \dfrac{1}{4}$

(5) $\dfrac{5}{10} - \dfrac{4}{10} = \dfrac{1}{10}$

(6) $\dfrac{5}{10} - \dfrac{4}{10} = \dfrac{1}{10}$

(7) $\dfrac{5}{10} - \dfrac{2}{10} = \dfrac{3}{10}$

(8) $\dfrac{2}{4} - \dfrac{2}{4} = 0$

(9) $\dfrac{9}{12} - \dfrac{4}{12} = \dfrac{5}{12}$

(10) $\dfrac{15}{20} - \dfrac{6}{20} = \dfrac{9}{20}$

(11) $\dfrac{10}{20} - \dfrac{5}{20} = \dfrac{5}{20} = \dfrac{1}{4}$

(12) $\dfrac{4}{6} - \dfrac{3}{6} = \dfrac{1}{6}$

(13) $\dfrac{10}{30} - \dfrac{9}{30} = \dfrac{1}{30}$

(14) $\dfrac{4}{6} - \dfrac{3}{6} = \dfrac{1}{6}$

(15) $\dfrac{5}{10} - \dfrac{5}{10} = 0$

(16) $\dfrac{9}{10} - \dfrac{5}{10} - \dfrac{3}{10} = \dfrac{1}{10}$

(17) $\dfrac{4}{5} - \dfrac{1}{5} - \dfrac{1}{5} = \dfrac{2}{5}$

(18) $\dfrac{16}{20} - \dfrac{5}{20} - \dfrac{4}{20} = \dfrac{7}{20}$

(19) $\dfrac{4}{5} - \dfrac{2}{5} - \dfrac{1}{5} = \dfrac{1}{5}$

(20) $\dfrac{8}{10} - \dfrac{4}{10} - \dfrac{2}{10} = \dfrac{2}{10} = \dfrac{1}{5}$

(21) $\dfrac{24}{30} - \dfrac{10}{30} - \dfrac{9}{30} = \dfrac{5}{30} = \dfrac{1}{6}$

(22) $\dfrac{8}{10} - \dfrac{5}{10} - \dfrac{2}{10} = \dfrac{1}{10}$

(23) $\dfrac{12}{15} - \dfrac{5}{15} - \dfrac{3}{15} = \dfrac{4}{15}$

(24) $\dfrac{8}{10} - \dfrac{4}{10} - \dfrac{2}{10} = \dfrac{2}{10} = \dfrac{1}{5}$

(25) $\dfrac{8}{10} - \dfrac{5}{10} - \dfrac{1}{10} = \dfrac{2}{10} = \dfrac{1}{5}$

Multipying Fractions

1) $\dfrac{1 \times 1}{3 \times 2} = \dfrac{1}{6}$

2) $\dfrac{1 \times 2}{3 \times 4} = \dfrac{2}{12} = \dfrac{1}{6}$

3) $\dfrac{1 \times 9}{2 \times 10} = \dfrac{9}{20}$

4) $\dfrac{1 \times 9}{4 \times 10} = \dfrac{9}{40}$

5) $\dfrac{1 \times 3}{2 \times 5} = \dfrac{3}{10}$

6) $\dfrac{3 \times 3}{4 \times 5} = \dfrac{9}{20}$

7) $\dfrac{3 \times 2}{10 \times 5} = \dfrac{6}{50} = \dfrac{3}{25}$

8) $\dfrac{2 \times 2}{4 \times 5} = \dfrac{4}{20} = \dfrac{1}{5}$

9) $\dfrac{2 \times 2}{4 \times 5} = \dfrac{4}{20} = \dfrac{1}{5}$

10) $\dfrac{9 \times 1}{10 \times 3} = \dfrac{9}{30} = \dfrac{3}{10}$

11) $\dfrac{2 \times 2}{5 \times 10} = \dfrac{4}{50} = \dfrac{2}{25}$

12) $\dfrac{3 \times 2}{4 \times 3} = \dfrac{6}{12} = \dfrac{1}{2}$

13) $\dfrac{1 \times 1}{4 \times 2} = \dfrac{1}{8}$

14) $\dfrac{1 \times 6}{2 \times 10} = \dfrac{6}{20} = \dfrac{3}{10}$

15) $\dfrac{2 \times 3}{5 \times 4} = \dfrac{6}{20} = \dfrac{3}{10}$

16) $\dfrac{8 \times 8}{10 \times 1} = \dfrac{64}{10} = \dfrac{32}{5} = 6\dfrac{2}{5}$

17) $\dfrac{1 \times 3}{10 \times 1} = \dfrac{3}{10}$

18) $\dfrac{2 \times 8}{10 \times 1} = \dfrac{16}{10} = \dfrac{8}{5} = 1\dfrac{3}{5}$

19) $\dfrac{2 \times 2}{5 \times 1} = \dfrac{4}{5}$

20) $\dfrac{2 \times 6}{4 \times 1} = \dfrac{12}{4} = \dfrac{3}{1} = 3$

21) $\dfrac{2 \times 6}{4 \times 1} = \dfrac{12}{4} = \dfrac{3}{1} = 3$

22) $\dfrac{3 \times 8}{5 \times 1} = \dfrac{24}{5} = 4\dfrac{4}{5}$

23) $\dfrac{3 \times 7}{4 \times 1} = \dfrac{21}{4} = 5\dfrac{1}{4}$

24) $\dfrac{2 \times 9}{3 \times 1} = \dfrac{18}{3} = \dfrac{6}{1} = 6$

25) $\dfrac{1 \times 8}{2 \times 1} = \dfrac{8}{2} = \dfrac{4}{1} = 4$

Dividing Fractions

1. $\dfrac{21 \times 5}{10 \times 13} = \dfrac{105}{130} = \dfrac{21}{26}$

2. $\dfrac{19 \times 5}{4 \times 11} = \dfrac{95}{44} =$

3. $\dfrac{15 \times 5}{4 \times 16} = \dfrac{75}{64} =$

4. $\dfrac{11 \times 2}{3 \times 7} = \dfrac{22}{21} =$

5. $\dfrac{13 \times 2}{5 \times 9} = \dfrac{26}{45}$

11. $\dfrac{7 \times 3}{2 \times 13} = \dfrac{21}{26}$

12. $\dfrac{11 \times 5}{4 \times 14} = \dfrac{55}{56}$

13. $\dfrac{9 \times 3}{2 \times 10} = \dfrac{27}{20} = 1\dfrac{7}{20}$

14. $\dfrac{7 \times 5}{2 \times 12} = \dfrac{35}{24} = 1\dfrac{11}{24}$

15. $\dfrac{5 \times 5}{2 \times 18} = \dfrac{25}{36}$

6. $\dfrac{9 \times 5}{2 \times 22} = \dfrac{45}{44} = 1\dfrac{1}{44}$

7. $\dfrac{5 \times 3}{2 \times 10} = \dfrac{15}{20} = \dfrac{3}{4}$

8. $\dfrac{9 \times 3}{2 \times 14} = \dfrac{27}{28}$

9. $\dfrac{9 \times 3}{2 \times 14} = \dfrac{27}{28}$

10. $\dfrac{5 \times 2}{2 \times 5} = \dfrac{10}{10} = 1$

16. $\dfrac{6 \times 5}{1 \times 4} = \dfrac{30}{4} = \dfrac{15}{2} = 7\dfrac{1}{2}$

17. $\dfrac{1 \times 1}{2 \times 3} = \dfrac{1}{6}$

18. $\dfrac{8 \times 2}{1 \times 1} = \dfrac{16}{1} = 16$

19. $\dfrac{6 \times 10}{1 \times 1} = \dfrac{60}{1} = 60$

20. $\dfrac{7 \times 4}{1 \times 3} = \dfrac{28}{3} = 9\dfrac{1}{3}$

21. $\dfrac{3 \times 1}{10 \times 6} = \dfrac{3}{60} = \dfrac{1}{20}$

22. $\dfrac{7 \times 4}{1 \times 2} = \dfrac{28}{2} = \dfrac{14}{1} = 14$

23. $\dfrac{2 \times 1}{4 \times 9} = \dfrac{2}{36} = \dfrac{1}{18}$

24. $\dfrac{1 \times 1}{3 \times 2} = \dfrac{1}{6}$

25. $\dfrac{1 \times 1}{5 \times 4} = \dfrac{1}{20}$